LOOK

LOOK

Solmaz Sharif

poems

Graywolf Press

This publication is made possible, in part, by the voters of Minnesota through a Minnesota State Arts Board Operating Support grant, thanks to a legislative appropriation from the arts and cultural heritage fund, and through a grant from the Wells Fargo Foundation Minnesota. Significant support has also been provided by Target, the McKnight Foundation, the Amazon Literary Partnership, and other generous contributions from foundations, corporations, and individuals. To these organizations and individuals we offer our heartfelt thanks.

Published by Graywolf Press
250 Third Avenue North, Suite 600
Minneapolis, Minnesota 55401

www.graywolfpress.org

Published in the United States of America

ISBN 978-1-55597-744-3

2 4 6 8 9 7 5 3

Library of Congress Control Number: 2015953717

Cover art: Joseph Nicéphore Niépce, *View from the Window at Le Gras*

Contents

CODA

look — (*) In mine warfare, a period during which a mine circuit is receptive of an influence.

Dictionary of Military and Associated Terms
United States Department of Defense

I.

Look

It matters what you call a thing: *Exquisite* a lover called me.
  Exquisite.

Whereas *Well, if I were from your culture, living in this country,*
  said the man outside the 2004 Republican National
  Convention, *I would put up with that for this country;*

Whereas I felt the need to clarify: *You would put up with*
  TORTURE, *you mean* and he proclaimed: *Yes;*

Whereas what is your life;

Whereas years after they LOOK down from their jets
  and declare my mother's Abadan block PROBABLY
  DESTROYED, we walked by the villas, the faces
  of buildings torn off into dioramas, and recorded it
  on a handheld camcorder;

Whereas it could take as long as 16 seconds between
  the trigger pulled in Las Vegas and the Hellfire missile
  landing in Mazar-e-Sharif, after which they will ask
  Did we hit a child? No. A dog. they will answer themselves;

Whereas the federal judge at the sentencing hearing said
  *I want to make sure I pronounce the defendant's name
  correctly;*

Whereas this lover would pronounce my name and call me
  Exquisite and lay the floor lamp across the floor,
  softening even the light;

Whereas the lover made my heat rise, rise so that if heat
  sensors were trained on me, they could read
  my THERMAL SHADOW through the roof and through
  the wardrobe;

Whereas *you know we ran into like groups like mass executions. w/ hands tied behind their backs. and everybody shot in the head side by side. its not like seeing a dead body walking to the grocery store here. its not like that. its iraq you know its iraq. its kinda like acceptable to see that there and not—it was kinda like seeing a dead dog or a dead cat lying—;*

Whereas I thought if he would LOOK at my exquisite face or my father's, he would reconsider;

Whereas *You mean I should be disappeared because of my family name?* and he answered *Yes. That's exactly what I mean,* adding that his wife helped draft the PATRIOT Act;

Whereas the federal judge wanted to be sure he was pronouncing the defendant's name correctly and said he had read all the exhibits, which included the letter I wrote to cast the defendant in a loving light;

Whereas today we celebrate things like his transfer to a detention center closer to home;

Whereas his son has moved across the country;

Whereas I made nothing happen;

Whereas *ye know not what shall be on the morrow. For what is your life?* It is even a THERMAL SHADOW, it appears so little, and then vanishes from the screen;

Whereas I cannot control my own heat and it can take as long as 16 seconds between the trigger, the Hellfire missile, and *A dog.* they will answer themselves;

Whereas *A dog.* they will say: Now, therefore,

Let it matter what we call a thing.

Let it be the exquisite face for at least 16 seconds.

Let me LOOK at you.

Let me LOOK at you in a light that takes years to get here.

II.

During the war, we felt the silence in the policy of the governments of English-speaking countries. That policy was to win the war first, and work out the meanings afterward. The result was, of course, that the meanings were lost.

—MURIEL RUKEYSER

BATTLEFIELD ILLUMINATION   on fire
                           a body running

PINPOINT TARGET   one lit desk lamp
and a nightgown walking past the window

LAY down
      to sleep then
      to rest last night
      to waste before
      across a stretcher
      across a shoulder
      over a leg
      beneath an arm
      in a shroud
      in a crib
      on top of a car
      chained to a bumper
      beneath a bridge
      in town square
      in the fountain
      in the Tigris
      under water boiled from smart bombs
      in a cellar
      in backseat counting streetlamps strobing overhead
      under bomblets
      under tendrils of phosphorus
      in a burnt silhouette
      on a cot
      under a tent
      still holding your breath
      beneath dining table
      beneath five stories
      in a hole

CONTAMINATED REMAINS   wash hands before getting in bed
leave interrogation room before answering cell
teach your mouth to say
honey when you enter the kitchen

DAMAGE AREA   does not include night sweats
or retching at the smell of barbeque

DEAD SPACE   fridges full
after the explosion the hospital
places body parts
out back where crowds
attempt to identify those
who do not answer their calls
by an eyeball
a sleeve of a favorite shirt
a stopped wristwatch

DESTRUCTION RADIUS   limited to blast site
and not the brother abroad
who answers his phone
then falls against the counter
or punches a cabinet door

Safe House

SANCTUARY where we don't have to

SANITIZE hands or words or knives, don't have to use a

SCALE each morning, worried we take up too much space. I

SCAN my memory of baba talking on

SCREEN answering a question *(how are you?)* I would ask and ask from behind the camera, his face changing with each repetition as he tried to watch the football game. He doesn't know this is the beginning of my

SCRIBING life: repetition and change. A human face at the seaport and a home growing smaller. Let's

SEARCH my father's profile: moustache black and holding back a

SECRET he still hasn't told me,

SECTION of the couch that's fallen a bit from his repeated weight,

SECTOR of the government designed to keep him from flying. He kept our house

SECURE except from the little bugs that come with dried herbs from Iran. He gives

SECURITY officers a reason to get off their chairs. My father is not afraid of

SEDITION. He can

SEIZE a wild pigeon off a Santa Monica street or watch

SEIZURES unfold in his sister's bedroom—the FBI storming through. He said *use wood sticks to hold up your protest signs then use them in*

SELF-DEFENSE *when the horses come,* his eyes

SENSITIVE when he passes advice to me, like I'm his

SEQUEL, like we're all a

SERIAL caught on Iranian satellite TV. When you tell someone off, he calls it

SERVICING. When I stand on his feet, I call it

SHADOWING. He naps in the afternoon and wakes with

SHEETLINES on his face, his hair upright, the sound of

SHELLS (SPECIFY)—the sound of mussel shells on the lip of the Bosphorus crunching beneath his feet. He's given me

SHELTER and

SHIELDING, shown it's better to travel away from the

SHOAL. *Let them follow you* he says from somewhere in Los Angeles waiting for me. If he feels a

SHORT FALL he doesn't tell me about it.

Deception Story

Friends describe my DISPOSITION

as stoic. *Like a dead fish,* an ex said. DISTANCE

is a funny drug and used to make me a DISTRESSED PERSON,

one who cried in bedrooms and airports. Once I bawled so hard at the
border, even the man with the stamps and holster said *Don't cry. You'll be
home soon.* My DISTRIBUTION

over the globe debated and set to quota. A nation can only handle so many
of me. DITCHING

class, I break into my friend's dad's mansion and swim in the Beverly Hills
pool in a borrowed T-shirt. A brief DIVERSION.

My body breaking the chlorinated surface makes it, momentarily, my
house, my DIVISION

of driveway gate and alarm codes, my dress-rehearsed DOCTRINE

of pool boys and ping-pong and water delivered on the backs of sequined
Sparkletts trucks. *Over here,* DOLLY,

an agent will call out, then pat the hair at your hot black DOME.

After explaining what she will touch, *backs of the hands at the breasts and
buttocks,* the hand goes inside my waistband and my heart goes DORMANT.

A dead fish. The last *female assist* I decided to hit on. My life in the American
Dream is a DOWNGRADE,

a mere DRAFT

of home. Correction: it satisfies as DRAG.

It is, snarling, what I carve of it alone.

Special Events for Homeland Security

Leave your DOLLY at home—this is no INNOCENT PASSAGE. Ladies, bring your KILL BOX. Boys, your HUNG WEAPON. You will push WARHEAD MATING to the THRESHOLD of ACCEPTABILITY. Whether you're PASSIVE or on the HUNTER TRACK, there's a room for you. An exclusive MAN SPACE with over two-dozen HEIGHT HOLES and bitches in READY POSITION. Eat until you damn near CANNIBALIZE. There's nothing you CANNOT OBSERVE. We ask you follow our TWO-PERSON RULE in restricted areas. Otherwise, get your SIMULTANEOUS ENGAGEMENT on. Please come with a safe PASSWORD and a NICKNAME, we'll provide PENETRATION AIDS and RESTRAINTS. Guaranteed to make your SPREADER BAR SWELL.

Dear INTELLIGENCE JOURNAL,

Lovely dinner party. Darling CASUALTIES and lean
sirloin DAMAGE of the COLLATERAL sort.
Extended my LETTER OF OFFER AND ACCEPTANCE
to the DESIRED INTERNAL AUDIENCE, reaching
DESIRED EFFECT and DESIRED PERCEPTION . . .
a lengthy and essential PLANNING PHASE,
down to our party's seating chart where I perfectly
placed gentlemen to avoid a HOSTILE ENVIRONMENT . . .
showed great CONSTRAINT . . . CIVIL AFFAIRS.
A real CIVIL CENSORSHIP. Even when he dropped that MEGATON
WEAPON on me, coyly I promised:
wait until you taste the COUP DE MAIN!
He stayed! To think, nights ago I wished
DISENGAGEMENT. Following tonight, to the T,
I did as mother suggested: IDENTIFICATION, FRIEND OR FOE.
Turned out FRIEND . . .
(If you have found this, please stop reading now.)
We were FRIENDLY beneath the gazebo's LATTICE . . . a LOW VISIBILITY
OPERATION, which is what my OVER-THE-HORIZON
RADAR was telling me. The INTERPRETABILITY of . . .
well, INITIAL ASSESSMENT, really . . . just MARGINAL INFORMATION,
I know. I promise more later. But, still
a truly really important POINT OF NO RETURN . . .
Stepped out to ASSESS this AREA
OF INFLUENCE, to admire together the ARCHITECTURE,
share a DESIRED APPRECIATION of our
HOME
LAND that (fingers crossed!) we will build together . . .

FREE MAIL

My DUMMY, my DUMP,
FENDER and FIREBALL,
where are you now?
Too LATE to remember
what I meant to write.
In the fifties,
people carried cards
with conversation topics
appropriate between fallout shelters
and *Whites Only* signs.
I steer through hills of windmills
and an AIRFIELD of BOMBERS,
pigeon nests gathering
in the quiet engines.

•

On YouTube, Blackwater
agents MOP UP bad guys
from a Najaf roof
like they're staving off
zombies. "Fucking niggers"
one says. He reloads
as some let their barrels cool
against the ledge.
He cried when he saw
the video. His boys claim
he's not a racist. Love,
I've started to say such
senseless things: "I know
where he is coming from"
and "I'm just doing my job."

•

ANTITERRORISM experts are talking
about us again. Some news anchor
cussing during commercials.
I saw your wanted ad at the subway station.
I saw a young Taliban
but couldn't see past his beauty,
brows of an ancient RELIEF, to the tank
he was riding on.

     •

If you wish a picture:
the map in my dashboard
is outdated and missing
two states, my left arm browned
from hanging out the car window,
my right at noon, fingers drumming,
a flat highway cutting through
fields and fields and fields and
FIRES moving down the hills.

Force Visibility

Everywhere we went, I went
in pigtails
no one could see—

ribbon curled
by a scissor's sharp edge,
the bumping our cars

undertook when hitting
those strips
along the interstate

meant to shake us
awake. Everywhere we went
horses bucking

their riders off,
holstered pistols
or two Frenchies

dancing in black and white
in a torn-apart
living room,

on the big screen
our polite cow faces
lit softly

by New Wave Cinema
I will never
get into. The soft whir

of CONTINUOUS STRIP IMAGERY.
What is fascism?
A student asked me

and can you believe
I couldn't remember
the definition?

The sonnet,
I said.
I could've said this:

our sanctioned twoness.
My COVERT pigtails.
Driving to the cinema

you were yelling
This is not
yelling you corrected

in the car, a tiny
amphitheater. *I will*
resolve this I thought

and through that
RESOLUTION, I will be
a stronger compatriot.

This is fascism.
Dinner party
by dinner party,

waltz by waltz,
weddings ringed
by admirers, by old

couples who will rise
to touch each other
publicly.

In INTERTHEATER TRAFFIC
you were yelling
and beside us, briefly

a sheriff's retrofitted bus.
Full or empty
was impossible to see.

Break-Up

1. In detection by radar, the separation of one solid return into a number of individual returns which correspond to the various objects or structure groupings. This separation is contingent upon a number of factors including range, beam width, gain setting, object size and distance between objects.

[I like to think years apart, in the]

distance between objects
contingent on a number of factors

[before the moment I first saw you,
a scaffolding a city walks beneath,
I like to think
we walked into Masjid-e Imam
and sent our voices up into its mosaic domes
and heard them clap back to us in seven
divine echoes, that our voices became
a PERMANENT ECHO, that we called
our names up into a dome to hear]

the separation of one solid return

[as our names returned, names
not even a blip on their]

radar

[names]

which correspond

[to our obsessions, mine
which means *flower that never dies*
and yours for an archer

who launched his arrow
and its impossible]

range

[which mapped the ends of the Persian Empire]

       2. In imagery interpretation, the result of magnification or
      enlargement which causes the imaged item to lose its identity
      and the resultant presentation to become a random series of
      tonal impressions. Also called **split-up.**

[I loved you at lunch]

the result of magnification

[when the coffee kicked in and you
cut carrots into coins]

a random series

[for our salad, the satisfying, slow knocking
of the dull knife
against the cutting board
while I pretended to read
while I worshipped you
from the sofa, an]

enlargement which causes

[a slow pleasure
it was at least slow
how you moved, PATIENT and inefficient,
unemployable and something
older, a shopkeeper on a stool.
I like to think, years apart,]

split-up

[we walked into the bazaar and you bought
a pocket watch, that we walked
into Masjid-e Imam and looked
up into its mosaic domes]

a series of tonal impressions

[we sent our voice
up into to hear it return, hear it]

lose its identity

[in seven echoes—was it?—the knock
of your knife against the splintered
board. *Can you hurry
up?* I'd say
the way you, slow,
it was pleasure, turned me over
and started at the shoulders
then started at the heels,
your hands moving up, so]

the resultant presentation

[was I saw all
I would have to leave—
*I don't want to die
I won't be ready*
and you tried to soothe,
said you'd die first
as an ACT OF MERCY, you
who hear a knock
and rise slow to answer, while I,
I wonder is this before
their GUNS come, the slow knock
of your knife I left
to hurry the leaving]

split-up

[I know I am hurrying toward what
I didn't want,
I know what it's]

Also called

GROUND VISIBILITY

this mangy plot where

by now
only mothers still come,

only mothers guard the nameless dead

    •

and then sparingly

    •

these graves: the Place of the Damned

the prison: History's Dumping Ground

    •

Peepholes burnt through the metal doors

of their solitary cells,

•

just large enough
for three fingers to curl out
for a lemon to pass through
for an ear to be held against
for one eye then the other
to regard the hallway
to regard the cell and inmate

•

peepholes without a lens

so when the GUARD comes to inspect me,
I inspect him.

Touch me, you said.

•

And through that opening

I did.

DESIRED APPRECIATION

Until now, now that I've reached my thirties:
All my Muse's poetry has been harmless:
American and diplomatic: a learned helplessness
Is what psychologists call it: my docile, desired state.
I've been largely well-behaved and gracious.
I've learned the doctors learned of learned helplessness
By shocking dogs. Eventually, we things give up.
Am I grateful to be here? Someone eventually asks
If I love this country. In between the helplessness,
The agents, the nation must administer
A bit of hope: must meet basic dietary needs:
Ensure by tube by nose, by throat, by other
Orifice. Must fistbump a janitor. Must muss up
Some kid's hair and let him loose
Around the Oval Office. *click click* could be cameras
Or the teeth of handcuffs closing to fix
The arms overhead. There must be a doctor on hand
To ensure the shoulders do not dislocate
And there must be Prince's "Raspberry Beret."
click click could be Morse code tapped out
Against a coffin wall to the neighboring coffin.
Outside my window, the snow lights cobalt
For a bit at dusk and I'm surprised
Every second of it. I had never seen the country
Like this. Somehow I can't say yes. *This is a beautiful country.*
I have not cast my eyes over it before, that is,
In this direction, is how John Brown put it
When he looked out from the scaffold.
I feel like I must muzzle myself,
I told my psychiatrist.

> "So you feel dangerous?" she said.
> Yes.
> "So you feel like a threat?"
> Yes.
> Why was I so surprised to hear it?

Inspiration Point, Berkeley

Consider Kissinger:
      the honorary Globetrotter
            of Harlem who spins on fingertip
      the world as balloon, the buffoon
erected and be-plaqued here
      by the Rotary Club as evergreen
            and in this Peace Grove planted
      alongside Waldheim and Nixon,
Bush, Herbert Walker and Mother Theresa,
      one Pope, one Dalai Lama, one Doctor
            King; Kissinger who was the one
      the bunnies in Hugh's mansion voted
MILF and is named here in our great tradition
      of naming, as on the Anza Expedition
            the conquistadors dropped
      armored mission after armored mission after saints—
Luis Obispo, Francisco, etc.—up this western coast my lover
      and myself now, by cleared path, regard,
            hardly touching
each other or the invasive grasses
the conquistadors also brought perhaps
      by bootsole, perhaps by taste as we like
            to do: to tote and plant and raze a home
we can recognize, even when we want anew, we two
invaders who love to recognize each other by shoulderstoop,
      by tone behind closed door or down
            beyond the trail bend, and so the grasses
      are Mediterranean, as were the Spanish
and what was before their former windows, as is *vista*
      point, which is where we are asked to stand
            to see before us land
      unnamed, and imagine ourselves, we twin Adams,
as the didactics at the trailhead suggest, witnessing the native
      flora that, before eucalyptus and other
            pacification, flourished

here, didactics that provide a painted rendition
of the lands, wildflowered and alive, before the Spanish came
and we came behind them and there is not
a one
in the painting—not a bowl or blanket,
not a toe or term of endearment, not a mother,
not a swimmer in the painted pre-Spanish San Pablo
Creek, though there are realistically rendered
salmon. There is nothing
that has nothing to do with this.

Dependers/Immediate Family

for Amoo

At the WWII Memorial, FDR thanks women
for sacrificing their sons
and their nylons.
Mothers oil supply lines

of parachutes
and what weighs chutes down,

sailing toward tall grass or rock,

a sky delivered by God.
I'm told to say it plain:

you did not want to fight,
but family sent you to the frontline,

sons in NEATLINES, ON-CALL for the Lord.

Your crib, your teddy bears,
I want to say mother put a GUN
there, blocks and blocks of boys
with pistols in their lunch pails,

lined up at the Army Experience Center
playing Call of Duty beneath the pacing of recruiters,
shit-talking into microphones in select US malls
while mothers shop the bed linens or grind coffee, grateful
for the quiet home, for the empty backyards

where boys would slam plastic cars together, their lips buzzing
like copter blades. Boys, they dream

of invisibility suits, explosive inks,
then grow up to work
in weapons research labs,

formulating rays to knock you out,
rays to make you puke, rays to activate
each nerve ending, gas to make you laugh

and boil. A soldier told me about *non-lethal weapons.*

He told me about the innards he scooped
then sewed
(with what)
up the toddler and the smell
of copper.

I am older than you'll ever be

and I keep going in that direction,
older than the boys

printed on state money
after going missing
in the smoke, beneath a tank,
the boys on a sun-faded, car-sooted mural
a wreath of white roses,
our precious, our cheapest
form of MINESWEEPING.

I'm now old enough to hear:
someone has to identify and
someone removes the shrapnel
and someone says not a scratch
when they pulled you out the fridge.

I imagine my father

looking into your cool face,
the difficult work of his knees

staying locked in that frozen place.

STATELESS PERSON

Our phone would
rarely ring. I have no ear
      for the mu-
      sic here. They would
bury one then another, the eldest son dropping
in

the grave to
comfort the corpse, calling us
        months later
        because we were
exiles, were vagabonds, fugitives, past Sierras,
past

oil rigs
in Texas, or waiting for
      the windshield
      to clear of frost,
two expanding ovals where the Buick's heat hit, our
eyes

opened to
kudzu, here where the dead can
      not reach us.
      Three thimbles with
her sweat, in the dresser drawer they emptied would, I bet,
roll,

clink, tongueless.
Gauze of soot, of skin sifted
      off her where
      she scratched her head,
licked her thumb to lift page after thin onionskin page,
cloaks

her mantel.
Portrait of Imam Ali,
        dead husband,
        dead son. She stuffed
plastic bags into plastic bags, clouds of them, some stuffed
with

cash. She who
pled *Eat.* pled *Pray.* said *I pray
        for your soul.*
        fasted, said *Ask
Him,* never once talked of love, or, fondly, *My husband,*
still

would that I
could lick the dust that like—I
        think it's—mu-
        sic will not reach
us here, just wet my fingertip, run along inside
one

sock drawer
so that her sugar, Shiraz
        bits she tracked
        inside, I could
eat, lick off her plastic tabletop whatever fell
grain

by grain off
her tiny, tin teaspoon. Where
        her gold went,
        who gives a shit.
I claimed her sugar bowl, white floral veil she prayed in,
to

take once her
daily, daily things. Morning
      (one, even)
      to step up her
thinly carpeted steps, hear her dentures click and clap.
I

can't hear that
music here.

FAMILY OF SCATTERABLE MINES

Suitcases of dried limes, dried figs, pomegranate paste,
parsley laid in the sun, burnt honey, sugar cubes hardened
on a baking sheet. Suitcases of practical underwear,
hand-washed, dried on a door handle, stuffed into boxes
from Bazaar-e Vakeel, making use of the smallest spaces,
an Arcoroc tea glass. One carries laminated prayers
for safe travel. I stand still when she smokes
esfand and fans away an evil eye. And when she asks
does this mean he will die? I say yes
without worrying it will break her. Suitcases
of fruit knives, of embossed boxes
with gold coins inside, the gaudiest earrings
brought for me, yellow, loud as these big women rolling meatballs
on the kitchen floor, lifting lit coals
with their fingers onto a head of tobacco.
Shisha comes from shisheh, which means glass.
Jigaram, they call me, which means my liver.
Suitcases they unpack and repack
over Iranian radio, between calls passing gossip,
the report on the brother's liver: it's failing, and he
doesn't want the sisters around because they will pray
and cry over him like he's already dead. Sisters unfurl
black shawls from suitcases to drape over their heads.
I carry trays of dates before the men, offer little
square napkins, thank their condolences, hold the matriarchs
while they rock. I answered yes when one asked,
does that mean he's going to die?

MASTER FILM

my mother around that blue porcelain,
my mother nannying around the boxed grits and just-add-water pantry
of the third richest family in Alabama,
my mother at school on Presbyterian dime and me
on my great grandmother's lap singing
her home, my mother mostly gone
and elsewhere and wondering
about my dad, my baba, driving a cab
in Poughkeepsie, lifting lumber in Rochester, thirtysomething
and pages of albums killed,
entire rows of classrooms
disappeared, my baba downing Bud Light by the Hudson
and listening to "Fast Car," my baba on VHS
interviewed by a friend in New York, his hair
black as mine is now, I'm four and in Alabama, I see him
between odd jobs in different states,
and on the video our friend shows baba a picture
of me and asks *how do you feel when you see Solmaz?*
and baba saying *turn the camera off* then
turn off the camera and then
can you please look away I don't want you to see my baba cry

Expellee

Chest films taken at the clinic. The doctor's softly
splintered popsicle stick. By five, I knew I was

a HEALTH THREAT. The daylong waits, the predawn lines.
Stale taste of toothpaste and skipped breakfast.

The *No* and *Next* metronome of INS. Numbered windows,
numbered tongues hanging out of red dispensers

you pull at the butcher shop. The ground meat left out
for strays, the sewing needles planted in it.

Mess Hall

Your knives tip down
in the dish rack
of the replica plantation home,
you wash hands

with soaps pressed into seahorses
and scallop shells white
to match your guest towels,
and, like an escargot fork, America,

you have found the dimensions
small enough to break
a man—
a wet rag,

a bullet, a bullet
like a bishop
or an armless knight
of the Ku Klux Klan,

the silhouette
through your nighttime window,
a quartet
plays a song you admire,

outside a ring of concertina wire
circles around a small collapse.
America, ignore the window and look at your lap:
even your dinner napkins are on FIRE.

Theater

I dropped down against the mosque wall
                              curled my shoulders in
let my feet fall apart
                    tilting toward the rubble-dusted floor
tried to still my lashes
                         as rifles came clanging in
their muzzles smelling out fear
                              heated off a pulse
I was playing dead
                         between the dead
a beast caught sight of my breath
                         blew off my face
said
              "Now he's fucking dead"

Soldier, Home Early, Surprises His Wife in Chick-fil-A

Soldier Surprises Family on the Field
During an NFL Game

"What a dramatic moment this is!"

Military Dad, Disguised as Captain America,
Surprises His Son on His Birthday

"What's wrong? What's wrong?
What happened? My buddy. My buddy."

Soldier, Hiding in a Box,
Surprises Daughter on Christmas

"You knew who I was. Right?"

Soldier Surprises Girlfriend
During Beauty Pageant, Then Proposes

"Sorry, ladies,
you're not getting an award like that."

Soldier Surprises Girlfriend at Baseball Game,
Then Proposes

"Wow! How 'bout that arm?"

Soldier, Home from Deployment,
Proposes to His Girlfriend Right Off the Airplane

"Of course."

After Being Welcomed Home,
Soldier Proposes to His Girlfriend

"What does that say?"

Vulnerability Study

your face turning from mine
to keep from cumming

8 strawberries in a wet blue bowl

baba holding his pants
up at the checkpoint

a newlywed securing her updo
with grenade pins

a wall cleared of nails
for the ghosts to walk through

Reaching Guantánamo

Dear Salim,

Love, are you well? Do they   you?
I worry so much. Lately, my hair   , even
my skin   . The doctors tell me it's   .
I believe them. It shouldn't
      . Please don't worry.
                    in the yard, and moths
have gotten to your mother's
                     , remember?
I have enclosed some   —made this
batch just for you. Please eat well. Why
did you   me to remarry? I told
          and he couldn't   it.
I would never   .
Love, I'm singing that   you loved,
remember, the line that went
"   "? I'm holding
the   just for you.

Yours,

Dear Salim,

Lightning across the sky all night, lighting up my   .
But no rain. No   .
When I get home, everything is
                              dust. One pair of
                by the   . One towel,
one   , one
in the morning. Anyway, I couldn't   ,
so I sat by the window watching
it streak   and
thinking I must look like something
lit up and   like this.

Yours,

Dear Salim,

At the store, they brought
         already, bruised on the
but still juicy. I pitted sour
         all day, the newspaper
went   with their juice. I save you
jars of preserves for your return.
         some plums, too. I haven't opened
a   since they
        you. Can't stand all those
   , all those   teeth. Or maybe
the   , how they stain upholstery like
  . I hope I don't make you   me.
I hope they allow you some   .

Yours,

Dear Salim,

                        said I need to
my tongue. It's getting sharp.
I told him to   his own
business, to   his own
wife. He didn't   .
If he wasn't my
I would never

                        again. Sometimes, I write you
letters I don't send. I don't mean
to cause alarm. I just want the ones
you open to
                        like a hill of poppies.

Yours,

Dear Salim,

                            have made a nest
under our   . And now
the nestlings always   .
The   of eggs has gone   .
And rice. And tea. I don't know who
decides   things.

Yours,

Dear Salim,

The neighbors got an apology
                    and a few thousand dollars.
They calculate   based on
              and
and age. The worth of a   , of a human
              .   hands shook as she opened
                    . She took it out front
and ripped it   .   a little pile
and set fire to it right there, right in front of

              .

              says they'll send me
a check   for   . I would
              !   !
                    ? Never.

Yours,

Dear Salim,

I read some   Hikmet,
Human   *Country*.
The wife sends letters to her
            like I do. I don't read
now. He was   like you.
I've   the books,
all of them. Can't stomach their
                              . All
those spines lined up on my shelf. How you
would stand there, smelling the pages.
            them. They all say
the same   story
and none tell ours.

III.

PERCEPTION MANAGEMENT
an abridged list of operations

ANTICA BABILONIA • BAGHDAD • BASTILLE • ABILENE • SUICIDE KINGS • GUN BARREL CITY • GOD HELP US (ALA ALLAH) • ARMY SANTA • CAVE DWELLERS • ROCK BOTTOM • PLYMOUTH ROCK • RAT TRAP • COWPENS • BAGHDAD IS BEAUTIFUL • BACKBREAKER • BLOCK PARTY • SWASHBUCKLE • SWARMERS • PUNISHER • BEASTMASTER • FLEA FLICKER • FIRECRACKER • LIGHTNING HAMMER • IRAQI HOME PROTECTOR • TOMBSTONE PILEDRIVER • BONE BREAKER • IRON REAPER • BELL HURRIYAH (ENJOY FREEDOM) • SPRING BREAK • ROCKETMAN • GLADIATOR • OUTLAW DESTROYER • DIRTY HARRY • GOLD DIGGER • UNFORGIVEN • RAGING BULL • THUNDERCAT • MR. ROGER'S NEIGHBORHOOD • SHADYVILLE • HICKORY VIEW • SCORPION STING • EAGLE LIBERTY • WOLFHOUND FURY • FALCON SWEEP • FALCON FREEDOM • SCALES OF JUSTICE • RAPIER THRUST • RELENTLESS HUNT • WOLF STALK • SWAMPFOX • TOMAHAWK • CRAZYHORSE THUNDER • GERONIMO STRIKE • PATRIOT STRIKE • QUICK STRIKE • RESTORING RIGHTS • CONSTITUTION HAMMER • INDUSTRIAL REVOLUTION • MONEY WORTH • RODEO • ALOHA • FOCUS • FLOODLIGHT • HARVEST LIGHT • RED LIGHT • RED BULL • PITBULL • BRUTUS • HERMES • SLEDGEHAMMER • GRIZZLY FORCED ENTRY • VACANT CITY • RIVERWALK • IRAQI HEART • RUBICON • RAMADAN ROUNDUP • GOODWILL • LITTLE MAN • ALKAMRA ALMANER (MOONLIGHT) • SALOON • STALLION RUN • LION HUNT • AL SALAM (PEACE) • JUSTICE REACH • ROCK REAPER • DEMON DIGGER • RAIDER HARVEST • IRON JUSTICE • UNITED FIST • WHITE ROCKETS • DONKEY ISLAND • BARNSTORMER • SOUK JADED (NEW MARKET) • CHURCH • CHECKMATE • KNOCKOUT • BACKPACK • SOCCER BALL • DOCTOR • THERAPIST • HELPING HAND • SCHOOL SUPPLIES • COOL SPRING • OPEN WINDOW • GLAD TIDINGS OF BENEVOLENCE

Personal Effects

> Like guns and cars, cameras
> are fantasy-machines whose use is addictive.
> —Susan Sontag

I place a photograph of my uncle on my computer desktop, which means I learn to ignore it. He stands by a tank, helmet tilting to his right, bootlaces tightened as if stitching together a wound. Alive the hand brings up a cigarette we won't see him taste. Last night I smoked one on the steps outside my barn apartment. A promise I broke myself. He promised himself he wouldn't and did. I smell my fingers and I am smelling his. Hands of smoke and gunpowder. Hands that promised they wouldn't, but did.

This album is a STOP-LOSS. By a dim lantern
or in the latrine
he flips through it.
He looks at himself
looking nearly as he does—
closest to himself then
as he could be, just learning
how to lean into his new body.
He suspends there
by STANDING ORDER,
a SPREADING FIRE in his chest,
his groin. He is on STAGE
for us to see him, see him?
He stands in the noontime sun.

A young soldier (pictured above) the son of an imam, brother to six, is among the latest casualties in the military campaign of Susangerd.

your whole body in a photo
your whole body
sitting on a crate
pressing your eyesocket
to the viewfinder
of a bazooka
crouched as you balance
the metal tube on your shoulder
in one you guide a belt of ammo
into the unfiring weapon
proud
your elbow out as if
mid-waltz
your frame strong
and lightly supporting the gun
a kind of smile
ruining the picture

You're posing. You're scared.
A body falls
and you learn to step over

a loosened head. You begin to appreciate
the heft of your boot soles,
how they propel you,

how they can kick in
a face—
the collapse

of a canopy bed
in an aerial bombardment,
mosquito netting doused

in napalm—cheekbones fragile
as moth wings beneath the heel.
You tighten your laces

until they hold together
a capable man.
Whatever rains,

the weight of your feet
swings you forward,
goose-stepping pendulums

a body less and less yours—
a body, God knows,
is not what makes you

anyway. So the hands
that said they never would
begin finding

grenade pins around their fingers,
begin flipping through this album
with soot under their nails.

you were not ready
But they issued the shovel and the rifle and you dug
But to watch you sitting there between the sandbags
But to watch the sand spilling out the bullet holes
But what did they expect
But what did they really think a sheet of metal could prevent
But I sat rolling little ears of pasta off my thumb like helmets
But it was not a table of fallen men
But my hand registered fatigue
But the men in fatigues were tired of sleeping in shifts
But you snuck into town and dialed home until you wrote your fingers
    were tired
But the code for Shiraz was down
But all of Shiraz was down
But the sheet lightning above the Ferris wheel of rusted bolts
But *I am sure they are alright* you wrote *Well* to reassure yourself
But the wind like an old mouth shaking the unnamed evergreen outside
    my window
But what I mean is I'd like very much to talk a bit

Hello

Operation Ramadan *was an offensive in the <u>Iran-Iraq War</u>. It was launched by <u>Iran</u> in July 1982 near <u>Basra</u> and featured the use of <u>human wave attacks</u> in one of the largest land battles since <u>World War II</u>.* **Aftermath**: *The operation was the first of many disastrous offensives which cost thousands of lives on both sides. This one in general boosted the casualty limit up to 80,000 killed, 200,000 wounded, and 45,000 captured. In retrospect, the Iranians lacked effective command and control, air support, and logistics to sustain an attack in the first place. Saddam Hussein offered several ceasefire attempts in the following years, none of which were accepted by the Revolutionary regime.*[6] [dead link]

Congratulations and condolences

They would say
That's the house of a martyr
pointing with their nose
That's the mother of a martyr

They are building a museum
for the martyrs.
Some metal shelf
a white archival box

with his PERSONAL EFFECTS.

I am attempting my own

myth-making.
He didn't want to have
anything

to do with it.
White-shrouded, they circled

his corpse, the ridge of his nose
peaking the sheet
or shaded by the boxlid,
around Shah Cheragh.

Daily I sit
with the language
they've made

of our language

to NEUTRALIZE
the CAPABILITY of LOW DOLLAR VALUE ITEMS
like you.

You are what is referred to as
a "CASUALTY." Unclear whether
from a CATALYTIC or FRONTAL ATTACK, unclear

the final time you were addressed

thou, beloved. It was for us a
CATASTROPHIC EVENT.

Just, DESTROYED.

DIED OF WOUNDS RECEIVED IN ACTION.

Yes, there was
EARLY WARNING.
You said you were especially scared
of mortar rounds.

In EXECUTION PLANNING, they weighed
the losses, the SUSTAINABILITY
and budgeted

for X number,
they budgeted for the phone call
to your mother and weighed that

against the amount saved in rations
and your taste for cigarettes

and the tea you poured your boys
and the tea you would've poured me
approaching *Hello.*

The change you collected in jars
jumping a bit
as the family learns to slam
the home's various doors.

How could she say
the things she does not
know. A poison

tipped arrow, she told
classmates at recess,
to the neck, hollow whistle

of it launched
from a blowgun
cutting the air between them.

According to most
definitions, I have never
been at war.

According to mine,
most of my life
spent there. Anthrax

in salt and pepper shakers,
patrol car windshields
with crosshairs painted over them,

some badge holding
my father's pocket contents
up to him and asking

where the cash is from.
The war in Iraq, I read,
is over now.

The last wheels gathering
into themselves
as they lift off

the sad tarmac. I say
begin. I say *end*
and you are to believe

this is what happens.
I say *chew 40 times*
before swallowing, slime,

and you go home to mother,
press a dog tag to your temple,
press a gun to that,

the tag flowering
into your skull. Thank God
for all-weather floor mats

and the slope of my personal driveway
and beer cans that change
color to let me know

they are cold enough.
The full-sized cab
smelling of iron and Axe body spray.

In 2003, a man held a fistful
of blood and brains to a PBS camera
and yelled

is this the freedom
they want for us? It was from his friend's
head. They were marching

as they figured Americans do.
Between them, hardly three horsepower
and still we shot him.

We say the war is over, but still
the woman leans across
the passenger seat

my son, my son.
I wasn't there
so I can't know, can I?

His mother's bed.
A grief we don't attempt to CONSOLE.

I killed him she'll tell me
years later. Fuck

CELESTIAL GUIDANCE.

I killed him she'll say
in the midst of CIVIL AFFAIRS

he surprises, he arrives,
eyes taped shut, torso held together
by black thread, fridge-cold—

       grief is a CLOSED AREA
     CLUTTERed with his fork against the plate
and other forgotten musics.

The enlarged ID photo above her mantel
means I can know Amoo,
my dear COLLATERAL DAMAGE,

as only a state or a school might do.

each photo is an absence,
a thing gone, namely
a moment, sometimes cities,
a tour boat balanced
on a two-story home
miles from shore

He was, we hope, moved.
Moved, but we will have to guess by what:

- shampoo in her wet hair
- salty and fried breads
- the chase scene in *Bullitt*
- sangak fresh from the oven dampening the newspaper on the walk home
  from the baker's
- the arms of someone who smells nice to him in the morning
- the mouth of someone laced with bergamot or cardamom, who dances
  in the kitchen and lets whatever's on the stove burn. Who burns for
  him

and beside him they burned,

they boiled, they fell,
shortly after a loud sound
that makes him piss himself.

- being nice to others
- loose change
- chess. He could beat all the brothers in chess.

He was moved like that
across a minefield—
moved by a hand we cannot see,

a hand that is all our hands combined.

at the bank
of some pond or salt marsh
tall grass
moustache
eyes closed
facing the sun
hands appear dead
by a fashion photographer's standard
your boots
like in the other photos
well worn
your nails square and closely cut
they are my nails
the army-issued belt
I would wear with Dickies
the army jacket
the Doc Martens
the military gear
that would stomp through my father's home
take that poster down my father said
it was Saddam in crosshairs
you are surrounded by the tall grass
and still I want to hiss
get down get down
so lit and tall
a stupid
thin helmet
between you and the gods

As Tolstoy wrote in a letter: *And yet, from nearby, all this wasn't at all as frightening as might be supposed . . . it was a question of who would burn the most powder, and at the very most 30 men were killed on both sides by these thousands of cannon shots . . .*

Or as I gleaned from your letters:

-

-

would, in Mashhad,

-

-

and my own broken Farsi.

-

-

freefall

-

-

then radio silence. An order

-

-

to disarm. *Stay.*

-

-

(December). They say move,

-

-

oil lamp. Two mines

-

-

as an anti-imperialist

-

-

tried to disarm, tried

-

-

maybe by the time you

-

-

Well. Ok. Sorry. I had

-

-

sorry. For this, I

-

-

By the time you

-

-

asking to bring you a camera,

an automatic please.

I search the cities where you were stationed

a ring of schoolboys
laid out on the plastic tarp
their crooked joints

a middle-aged man with
ground meat

where his foot used to be.
I looked
to see if I could find you

netting over your helmet.

In one letter,
you name the seventh killed
in your company

Well maybe I am next.
You didn't say much else

But it must have
He must have
To record the one name

and that being the name of a dead man

Ok. Bye for real
this time you signed off

on page 6.

His father grew very quiet
His father would
HEAVY DROP sob
behind a closed door

His father was
PERSON ELIGIBLE TO RECEIVE EFFECTS
A PILLBOX of opium
in his sock drawer

you hand
plucked wild poppies
to soldier friends
imagine the wetness
at the broken stem
me and two girls
at a Birmingham back fence
clearing almost
an entire vine of honeysuckles
that sugar
tasting vaguely of grass
carnage of petals
and pistils licked clean
at our little bee feet

What I see are your hands
peeling apples, the skin curling
to the floor in one long unravel,

a spit-up film reel
loosened from its canister, and
I'm not even sure they are apples, quince,

pear, some desert potato with a stem.
From the number of peels
I assume you are feeding

the other men in your tent.
Your head is down.
Maybe the cameraman

asked you to look at him
and you couldn't stomach
it. Maybe around you,

today, they fell until
you didn't understand
how you hadn't

been hit.
I decide you are happy
for the knife

in your hands,
the white dust
on your bare feet. I am happy

to see your bare feet
in this photo. They are
the only things that

made me cry. It's that
they existed
and that they, appalling,

look so dead already.
I think it's fair to say
you want to do something

with your hands, whether
or not the photographer
placed the apples in front of you

whether or not they are
apples, whether or not
earlier that day you saw

a friend's lungs peeking
out the back of his throat.
I cannot name

the weapons leaning
on the wall behind you—Kalashnikovs?
Howitzers?—as you write

a letter. I wrote
I burn my finger on the broiler
and smell trenches, my uncle

pissing himself. "How can she write that?
She doesn't know," a friend, a daughter
of a Vietnam vet, told another friend,

another daughter of a Vietnam vet.

it was his bare toes
that made me cry
because I realized then he had toes
and because dusted in the white
desert sand they looked
like a corpse's toes
while his hands worked off a peel
inches above the earth

Operation Nasr, *fought in early January 1981, was a major battle of the* <u>*Iran-Iraq War*</u>*. Three Iranian armored* <u>*regiments*</u> *advanced towards Iraqi forces who had invaded Iranian territory between the cities of* <u>*Ahvaz*</u>*,* <u>*Susangerd*</u>*, and* <u>*Dezful*</u>*.The Iraqi forces were alerted to this movement and feigned a withdrawal. The Iraqis formed three armored regiments into a three-sided box ambush. The Iranians blundered into the ambush and the two* <u>*tank*</u> *forces battled for four days in a sea of mud. The battle had been ordered by* <u>*President Abdulhassan Banisadr*</u> *who was hoping that a victory might shore up his deteriorating political position; instead the failure of the offensive helped to hasten his fall.*[26]

I write him daily

And so I learn to ignore him

And so I begin to list pocket contents as if filing an autopsy report

And I place in his hands a metal tongue of a fly

And I place in his hands a metal tongue of a tank control board

And I place in his hands a Bic lighter and loose leaf paper

And I place in his hands a trigger, a shutter

And still not even a bar of his laughter

And by April the script in his letters grew tighter, barbed, men in a shoulder-
     width trench

And when I sounded out M-EE-N to mean *mine* a hole appeared in the letter
     and I couldn't look at it

And I drove into pothole after pothole

And I drove past a hundred balloons held down in a net

And gone even the netting over his helmet

And alive we bring up the hands to hold together his neck

And I place in his hands his head

And I place in his hands my hands

And I place in his eyes a LOOK we share in the rearview

And I place between us a bar of laughter

And I place between us the looking and the telling they want dead

Amoo,

In a tarot card reading
A asks "Are you open
to love? Are you keeping love in mind?"

Amoo, I think.
Amoo.
The word a moan

a blown kiss
the soft things it makes a mouth do.
Amoo, I thought

as he told me about the Page of Cups,
the echo of what
I've never called you.

Hello you'd approach
in the international terminal.
I'd be disheveled

from the search, raw.
Hello. Do you know who I am?
Amoo Javad I'd say.

The things a mouth wishes to
Amoo jan
or Amoo Javad

or Amoo joon Javad
Janam you would respond—
My life, my soul, you'd say—

Language and its expectations
teaches us
about the relationship

we would have had.
Na kheyr, for example—
that we need words

for refusal makes it likely
we would refuse things
of each other.

Or *Baleh.* As in you say
Do you know who I am
and I respond,

though you could be a number of brothers
from our albums,
Yes.

I wrote
I burn my finger on the broiler
and smell trenches, my uncle

pissing himself. How can she write that?
She doesn't know.

As if a film projection caught
in theater dust, I play it

out: I approach you

in the new Imam Khomeini Airport,

fluorescent-lit linoleum, you walk up
to meet me, both palms
behind your back
like a haji. You stoop, extend a hand

Hello. Do you know who I am?

Yes, I tell you, I half-lie,
Yes. An address, beloved
lit
a rooftop of doves

        crouched to launch
Yes, Amoo.

How could I not?

CODA

*. . . Let this be the Body
through which the War has passed.*

—FRANK BIDART

DRONE

:   somewhere I did not learn *mow down* or *mop up*

:   somewhere I wouldn't hear *your father must come with me* or *I must fingerprint your grandmother can you translate please*

:   the FBI has my cousins' computers

:   my father says *say whatever you want over the phone*

:   my father says *don't let them scare you that's what they want*

:   my mother has a hard time believing anything's bugged

:   my father and I always talk like the world listens

:   my father is still on the bus with contraband papers under his seat as uniforms storm down the aisle

:   it was my job to put a cross on each home with dead for clearing

:   it was my job to dig graves into the soccer field

:   I wrote *red tracksuit*

:   I wrote *Shahida headless found beside Saad Mosque buried in the same grave as the above*

:   I wrote *unidentified fingers found inside Oldsmobile car*

:   I wrote their epitaphs in chalk

:   from my son's wedding mattress I know this mound's his room

:   I dropped a knee and engaged the enemy

:   I emptied my clip then finished the job

:   I took two steps in and threw a grenade

:   I took no more than two steps into a room before firing

:   in Haditha we cleared homes Fallujah-style

:   my father was reading the Koran when they shot him through the chest

:   they fired into the closet

:   the kitchen

:   the ninety year old

:   the stove

:   just where was I

:   *una a una tu cara en todos los buses urbanos*

:   *Here lie the mortal remains of one who in life searched your face*

:   call me when you get home

:   let's miss an appointment together

:   let's miss another flight to repeated strip searches

:   that Haditha bed with magenta queen sheets and wood-shelved headboard and blood splattered up the walls to the ceiling

: they held each other

: they slept on opposing ends wishing one would leave

: mother doesn't know who I am anymore

: I write *Mustapha Mohammad Khalaf 15 months old*

: I write *Here lies an unknown martyr a big security guard with a blue shirt found near an industrial area with a chain of keys*

: *Martyr unknown only bones*

: they ask if I have anything to declare then limit my response to fruits and nuts

: an American interrupts an A and B conversation to tell me *you don't have to do anything you don't want to do*

: he strikes me as a misstep away from *she was asking for it*

: what did you expect after fishing Popov from a trash bin

: what did you expect after accepting a marbled palace

: they drag the man who killed my uncle out a hole

: they inspect him for ticks on national television

: no one in my family celebrates

: when the FBI knocks I tell them *I don't have to do anything I don't want to do* and they get a kick out of that

: she just laid there and took it like a champ

:   she was dying for it

:   at a protest a man sells a shirt that reads *My dick would pull out of Iraq*

:   my mother tape-records my laugh to mail bubblewrapped back home

:   my mother records me singing *Ye shabe mahtab mah miad to khab*

:   I am singing the moon will come one night and take me away side street by side street

:   sitting on a pilled suburban carpet or picking blue felt off the hand-me-down couch

:   the displaced whatnots

:   I practice the work of worms

:   how much I can wear away with no one watching

:   two generations ago my blood moved through borders according to grazing and seasons

:   then a lifeline of planes

:   planes fly so close to my head filled with bomblets and disappeared men

:   scaffolding sprouts nooses sagging with my dead

:   I burn my finger on the broiler and smell trenches

:   my uncle pissing himself

:   shopping bags are legs there is half a head in the gutter

:   I say *Hello NSA* when I place a call

:   somewhere a file details my sexual habits

:   some tribunal may read it all back to me

:   Golsorkhi, I know the cell they will put me in

:   they put me onto a crooked pile of others to rot

:   is this what happens to a brain born into war

:   a city of broken teeth

:   the thuds of falling

:   we have learned to sing a child calm in a bomb shelter

:   I am singing to her still

Notes

Terms appearing in small caps are taken from the United States Department of Defense's *Dictionary of Military and Associated Terms* as amended through October 17, 2007. As a supplement to standard English dictionaries (e.g., Merriam-Webster), this military dictionary is updated regularly, often monthly, with unclassified terms being added and subtracted as needed. Need is determined by a combination of factors, including military usage, presence of the term in standard English, etc. For example, the term "drone" appeared in the 2007 version, but no longer appears in the 2015 version. It is likely "drone" was removed from the dictionary since understanding of the term has fully entered English vernacular; in other words, the military definition is no longer a *supplement* to the English language, but the English language itself. Given the impossibility of keeping up with changes in the dictionary, I have used the October 17, 2007, edition throughout. This edition has over 5,900 terms, only a fraction of which appear in these poems. Some of the terms that do not appear here despite my efforts include:

> *absolute dud; beaten zone; crush depth; dazzle; enemy combatant; force beddown; guinea-pig; half-life; imitative communications deception; Joint Worldwide Intelligence Communication System; kite; light damage; minefield lane; nuisance minefield; operational art; proper authority; rainfall (nuclear); religious support; salted weapon; touchdown zone; unwarned exposed; very seriously ill or injured; war game; weapons of mass destruction; zone of action; zone of fire*

The line *una a una tu cara en todos los buses urbanos* in "DRONE" is taken from Leonel Rugama's "Epitafio."

Acknowledgments

Poems from this collection have appeared in the following publications:

American Poets: Soldier, Home Early, Surprises His Wife in Chick-fil-A
Black Warrior Review: Break-Up
Boston Review: Safe House
DIAGRAM: Lay
Granta: Force Visibility
Gulf Coast: Dependers/Immediate Family; Master Film
jubilat: Contaminated Remains; Free Mail
The Kenyon Review: Desired Appreciation; Inspiration Point, Berkeley;
     Personal Effects
Lit Hub: Stateless Person (under the title "Exile Elegy")
The New Republic: Perception Management
Paper Bag: Reaching Guantánamo
PBS Tehran Bureau: Family of Scatterable Mines (under the title
     "Suitcases"); Theater
PEN Poetry Series: Look
PN Review: Reaching Guantánamo
Poetry: Vulnerability Study; Ground Visibility (under the title "Lanat
     Abad / The Place of the Damned")
Sink Review: Special Events for Homeland Security; Dear
     Intelligence Journal,
Witness: Drone

This book exists because of a series of generosities, personal and professional. Sincere thanks to the Poetry Foundation, the Rona Jaffe Foundation, the Fine Arts Work Center in Provincetown, the 92Y, the MacDowell Colony, Bread Loaf Writers' Conference, the Kenyon Review Writers Workshop, National Endowment for the Arts, VONA/Voices of Our Nation, the Creative Writing Program at NYU, and the Creative Writing Program at Stanford University for time, resources, and ceaseless faith.

To my teachers: Eavan Boland, D. A. Powell, Ken Fields, W. S. DiPiero, Ruth Forman, Jen Scappettone, Junichi Semitsu, Breyten Breytenbach,

Phillis Levin, Matthew Rohrer, Deborah Landau, Major Jackson, Yusef Komunyakaa, and Sharon Olds.

Thank you to David Baker, Ken Chen, Timothy Donnelly, Cathy Park Hong, Persis Karim, Don Share, who straddle many of these categories—and all the anonymous readers, editors, and judges for their early faith and advocacy. Thank you to Jeff Shotts for realizing this book.

More friends, mentors, family than can be named, but especially to these heroes for the conversations and comments: Golnar Adili, Ari Banias, Luis Bocaletti, Cathy Linh Che, Colin Cheney, Arash Davari, Natalie Díaz, Tarfia Faizullah, Meg Glasson, Suheir Hammad, Janine Joseph, Fady Joudah, Shoaib Kamil, Christopher Kempf, Rickey Laurentiis, Ricardo Maldonado, John Murillo, Alberto Palomar, Maisha Quint, Roger Reeves, Sam Ross, Arash Saedinia, Mrigaa Sethi, Brandon Som, Bianca Stone, R.A. Villanueva, Ocean Vuong, Phillip B. Williams, and the ineffable Samira Yamin.

I carry June Jordan's Poetry for the People, June herself and the family therein, with me everywhere. Love—especially to marcos ramírez, who didn't let me run.

To my parents, Afsaneh and Saeed—for their courage, their righteousness. And the scrappy family we've made—Naz, Nima, Bijan, Behrooz, Farah, Mohammad, Parivash, Said, Sanaz, Peiman, Sasan, Parvin, Soroush, Hanna, Manzar—wherever we've found ourselves.

This book is in immeasurable memorium.

SOLMAZ SHARIF holds degrees from the University of California, Berkeley, where she studied and taught with June Jordan's Poetry for the People, and New York University. She has been selected to receive a Rona Jaffe Writer's Foundation Award, a Ruth Lilly and Dorothy Sargent Rosenberg Fellowship, and a fellowship from the Fine Arts Work Center in Provincetown. Her work has appeared in *Granta,* the *New Republic, Poetry,* and elsewhere. A former Stegner Fellow, she is currently a Jones Lecturer in Poetry at Stanford University. This is her first collection.

The text of *Look* is set in Adobe Garamond. Composition by Bookmobile Design & Digital Publisher Services, Minneapolis, Minnesota. Manufactured by Versa Press on acid-free, 30 percent postconsumer wastepaper.